Lost
Gospels

Lost
Gospels

Lorri
Neilsen
Glenn

*miranda —
best wishes
on your
journeys in
writing
— Lorri
2010*

Brick Books

Library and Archives Canada Cataloguing in Publication

Neilsen Glenn, Lorri
    Lost gospels / Lorri Neilsen Glenn.

Poems.
ISBN 978-1-894078-77-1

    I. Title.

PS8577.E3373L67 2010   C811'.6   C2009-907179-7

We acknowledge the Canada Council for the Arts, the Government of Canada through the Book Publishing Industry Development Program (BPIDP), and the Ontario Arts Council for their support of our publishing program.

The cover image is a photograph of the Ponte Vecchio in Florence, taken by the author.

The author photograph was taken by Allan Neilsen.

The book is set in Minion and Trade Gothic.

Design and layout by Alan Siu.

Printed and bound by Sunville Printco Inc.

Brick Books
431 Boler Road, Box 20081
London, Ontario N6K 4G6

www.brickbooks.ca

Contents

Lost gospels

Verge

Learning the words

Songs for Simone

Just so you know

Comes a time

Lost gospels

Lost gospels

1.

The true earthly blessings are metaxu...the temporal seen as a bridge. Simone Weil

You know, it's possible to invent anything: a soul, flight, the barrelhouse blues
on a Saturday night, where you'd be today if you'd turned left out of the door

and not the other way. God save your dreams. And your hands, those compass
needles that quiver with applause for the light. But remember: no figure

of speech is bright enough to light your way home. Open your throat before
the sun pulls down the afternoon, and the leaky boat of language leaves

the safety of the shore. Start by naming everything you tried to resist:
the blood red road, her willing breast, the North Star, the trigger of a gun,

or the arms of The Good Book; his hands cooling on the white sheet, veined
as snow-stung leaves lifting and settling into the speckled ground. You know

sorrow is memory's sister; everything calls out your name. Next, don't
underestimate the whirling forces of once-upon-a-time. Here's one: a man steals

his brother's flock, but charms himself into favour again with the fetching sounds
he can make from the hollows of reeds. Everybody plays the fool, you know—

Anansi knows, and Coyote and Raven, and they rummage your house at night
for shiny trinket tales, aided and abetted by the rhythm of the moon. Or there's

the one about Mahalia, rebuked and scorned, or a man named Willie Johnson
blinded at seven, and they sang, oh yes, they raised light from dark water, dug

diamonds out of the cold, cold ground. And once upon the strains

of the rolling prairie, a stone angel and a song for the song of Piper Gunn.
Hungry cries from the boreal plain and a song for the river that runs

behind you and will run beyond. Dry lips and northern Ontario and blue blue
windows, your urge for going, the early morning rain, the train you were going

to ride. Or the legacy of a grandfather, a Nisei shipped to Alberta to plant
sugar beets, the thrumming of the war, how he bore it all with a quiet grace

that hums in your limbs, a melody as pure as you are ever going to hear.
So ask yourself: when desire strums you like a fingerboard, what else can you

feel but faith, how it resonates? Listen: you are the meantime. Walk into the water,
and when the vibration summons your bones, you know you're coming home.

Let yourself burst into the silence, follow your hands, those fishes of wonder.
Dodge the swirling foam, the net, the rocks, dodge this metaphor, reach

for the one true note that shudders, the story you cannot resist. It will find you
and it will enter you. It will make you. It will make you. Sing.

2.

Sunday morning. The sun assaults your eyes. Birds in the trees are quiet.
A robin bounces on the barren patch at the corner by Main Street, foxtail barley

fringes the road, twirls its hair when the wind rises. On the perimeter, dust rolls
like regret behind the wheels of a car heading east. Above, a cabbage butterfly;

two. Then another two: Danceland for fliers. Main Street scours
itself in baked emptiness, bony shadows pooling on one side. Ahead,

a new red F-150 outside a tiny house, a large rag on the windshield, but no
water, no hose nearby. Everything still. On the gravel, a rusted barbecue

and three Kokanee empties near a pale, stained lawn chair. Your steps
slow. No, it is not a rag. Pinned carefully, evenly, under the blade of the wiper

against the glass are two brown speckled wings. You see under the feathers
the shield is cracked, the head of the Swainson's twisted around, down,

as you have twisted coat hangers you meant to discard, the white
of breast and belly thrust into morning like the prow of a prairie ship.

3.

Heat bears down on the dust, parses birdsong in the ditch. Sparks of wild blue
flax, a band of hawkweed along the road. You can get by on a few nouns here, and
verbs are regular as an eight-hour shift or the liver and onions at the hotel. In the
evening, mufflers argue with mowers and dogs, the young learn new words for
the highway out of town, and crows—those orators of razz—pick in the gravel for
a lingo they'll claim as their own.

4.

Together you walk into the open field of prairie wool
toward the ravine, its scattered harvest of old combines, rusted

limbs locked in a last plié, pocked and peeling and fired
by the sun. Here grass is flattened in the shape of animal belly,

an owl bursts from under the metal to write
explosion in feathers against the hill. A mule fawn,

her ears like questions, her bounding
answer. The doe, and along the horizon, the buck,

alone and unreadable, striding from
shelter in such a way you know he knows and is

gone. Below, blooming, a member of the aster
family; one of you calls, as the other stoops to look

at the pink, the yellow, then blue. It has become
a joke between you—these small encroachments

you make, words in cupped palms, cradles for carrying
an image home, tucking it under the joists and beams

of language, safe, at least for now. A leaf,
a petal you can point to in a book, one of the *Asteraceae*,

its twenty thousand species, surely it is listed.
Near the flesh of your feet, the rubbed

grass, a badger hole, a magpie, its white flash.
An old story, and long: the prairie's sere

rough gospel, ragged, scrabbling, good news
that slips between the names.

5. ·

You are home. Not home. Impossible
to navigate the liminal. A friend says:
After forty years I still see the same you. Who is this she sees?
The bow of this skiff carries you into the present and cuts
time: you cannot tell
wake from ocean, vessel from the arc of horizon.
Float: the past is foam,
it drenches.

6.

You turn off the radio—Lebanese children bombed, a flood,
an earthquake, the eightieth Canadian soldier gone, and the planet
keening its bitter, particular strains out of old ice, air, cracks

in its simmering core. When you open the door, a moth flies
at your hair. You raise an arm to sweep it away, and it falls
on the wooden stoop. A small shadow has never seemed so heavy,

redemption so improbable. The clang of metal, a crash: the man
next door, bare-chested, has thrown a small orange tricycle
against the fence. He roars his fury until it splits

the air into small, sharp barbs that seem briefly to clear
the pickets, rise beyond the elm, Main Street, and the highway
out of town, across fields of canola, along the hobbled

green humps of the Qu'Appelle, above the shaggy plain
where they will swarm and churn with other piercing
frequencies, and coalesce.

7.

…but of sea half is earth, half lightning storm. Herakleitos

Bargaining faith for sleep, you see light stir at the window, white
hissing above the crow-knuckled elms, exposing the wet furrows

of the seeded fields cooling after the longest day of the year.
The turning. Air thickening electric, forks bulging with spark. Imagine

an axe behind the clouds, splitting the moon apart for stars. Always,
there is sacrifice. Rising on sea legs you watch the aspen convulse

under buckled air, and you ride; water, wind, light thrash
and you ride the swell, hollow as a gourd, a cup emptied

of any purpose but this: to be drenched in stupefied gratitude.
Always, there is a gift. In the morning, green leaves

drying like tears on the field. The sun and your footfall, new.
A killdeer, shrieking.

8.

I come…like the swallow that perches light-footed in the fore-part of your house. Homer

Kay reaches under the side table, behind the doilies and the crocheted
dishcloths. *I want you to see these albums, so you know who's who.* Kamsack.
The last century. Before she has set the scrapbooks on the table, your body
is awake with the lost extravagance of what cannot be photographed.

The sway of rhubarb and the scissor-clip flight of butterflies. How you dug in
that garden under thistle and chickweed to find warrens of worms, beetles,
perhaps ghosts of seeds sprouted, realized in the blood of those who tended,
cooked, pickled, put up, as Eleanore did, and of those, too, like Charlie or Kay
whose mouths rode the taste of orange, red, green, yellow the way you float hope,
crane toward morning.

And the tales of raspberries, those jeweled and hairy soothsayers. Never again
the glamorous indolence of sweet peas, their folded hands of pink and blue
clinging to sticks and string, your fingers on their flesh. Your uncle from Seattle,
smelling of tobacco and Brylcreem, how he whispered: *See these shears?*
Take one more flower and your ear is gone.

Her album cannot hold images of the empire of sunflowers, those proud
descendants of the golden helmet high above the tomato plants. How their
heads follow the sun to the east. Spits they produced, Duke
seeds they were called then, named for Freedomites your grandfather
swore marched buck naked in the street, people whose resilience
you learn later, built this region.
                              You felt small
beside the burly stocks, and later, when frost invaded,
helpless. The shame in their drooping heads.

This light-footed, untethered flickering, these orphans of meaning that land
in the forefront, then disappear. A driveway created from tires erasing grass.
Across the way, a funeral home on the corner lot. By the building, old dog limp
in the heat, sighing. You ventured, retreated: his teeth, the funk of matted fur.

And lilies, at the edge. Tigers in the lane, eyeing you. You wanted to be that brash.

These flashes are traces in your blood, cannot be shown. Kay's hand trembles, lifts
the leaves of her book, narrates what you never knew. *Here is the house being built
in 1912, before the garden,* she says. *And here is one of Trixie with Elvin, one in his
Air Force uniform—before the cyclone—another with the six of them—after Elaine left
and before Iona had moved to the city to stay with an aunt. One of you and your grandmother,*
Kay says, nudging you—*Eunice introduced your father and mother in Kamsack,
did you know that?*

She lifts the plastic, pulls out a paper. *Elaine's birth certificate. Elaine Irene Anna Boggs,
born 30th of May, 1917. Parents' marriage: Selkirk, Manitoba. June 28, 1919.* The dates
don't work, but you do not mention this. What's done is set adrift.

As is the scab on your knee, your brown arms, the sour taste of dandelion milk,
a rain barrel, that song, a sun-cracked screen door. The wild bliss of being new,
unknowing.

On the table, a scattering of faces grey as seed heads. Kay's shadows will never be yours,
but she wants you to have them. Together and alone, you swirl with traces as dispersed
as the lost children of Mnemosyne. Kay's hands flit, perch lightly, here, there.

I'll be gone soon, she says: no hint of sorrow. *Look, this one is your dad's cousin—*

9.

The fan churns dry ghosts in this hot day, and you close
the chapter on Heidegger, reach for the light switch when, flailing

against the current of air, it appears. A force of faith: a knot, alive,
a tangle of black thread with wings, frail thing at the end

of summer. It must have fallen through the open screen, now
it's drunk and dizzied, as you are, by the downswirl of finding what

it does not know. Aletheia, you name it, and why not? An insect
exposed under the gaze of a sixty-watt bulb, lurching its way through

being and nothingness in a river of wave and particle, movement
and mass. Wanderer like you, shocked by the fathoming.

10.

Number is the cause of gods and demons. Seven is a perfect number. Pythagoras

Tears spring from sorrow
and from joy. You want clouds, heat,
bristling lightning.

Words are the sharpest
tools you can make. You load them
in guns, and wonder.

Red sun in the lake.
Cantankerous crows at dusk.
Being here is simple.

From nothing, you grew.
May you leave softly, the trace
of a bell ringing.

When you avoid dark,
you miss the beauty
of chiaroscuro.

Lost gospel scholars
say Judas was a true friend.
Search for all the songs.

Why not start over,
forget all of this doing?
Don't count. Just listen.

Verge

Sometimes lilies were so abundant that they covered an area of ground bright red.

Lilies followed her—or did she follow them?—into the foothills of the Rockies, by the Rosevear ferry, against the soles of her rubber boots as she held a jam pail and reached for blueberries large as thumbs, imagining in every bush-rustle an approaching bear. She saw blooms in ditches, sometimes took one home, but more often sat in the grass and held it: holy red chalice, Hera's wild colour, upright, anthers throbbing with pollen, those dark eyes a feral presence the child could not understand. All she knew was they were the answer to the question: What single thing do you love?

Lilies grow in a surprising variety of disturbed and undisturbed habitats...
they do not grow on land that has been cultivated.

In the back seat of the old grey Studebaker, alone in a family, she
rolled down the window, looked for what rose from the ashes of
burned thatch: beauty in the verge. Train towns whistled years
away—Saskatoon, Prince Albert, Kamsack, Edson, Dauphin, The Pas,
Winnipeg. She hid images at the back of each desk, school to school,
rendering them crudely with worn-down points of red and black and
yellow Laurentians. Everyone else chose roses or daisies from yards;
she searched for spears of red near sloughs, on the wayside, near
railway lines, on the shoulders of gravel roads. That bright
transparent flesh: how can it be?

A fire that occurs before the plants emerge can rejuvenate a lily population by stimulating growth in the flower shoots that have been waiting underground for years.

Nature loves to hide, says Herakleitos. She waited: under books, at crossroads, in crevices of lost opportunity. After storms, so many fires. The girl learned death, disruption, a longing to belong and not to belong, to reach out, to retreat. Every so often something rose under her ribs, a shoot of joy, and it opened its wings, tried to lift her out of the smoke. She was suspended, neither grounded nor in flight.

After the fire, the number of lilies was unbelievable—I have seen nothing like it before or since.

Colour in the hues of those sepals. Food and medicine for her Métis grandmother, a tea for fevers and childbirth. Patience during drought, blessing in the small chance of a rhizome: mother, child. Fifty years later, the girl searches for what is now rare: *pick none,* says the guidebook. Uncultivated areas are so few; hope, quiescent. A tiger story, lost and necessary. Where is the wild? A singular belief? Feral love?

Learning the words

Lucy: A love story about daughters

1. Once upon a time in the beginning

you couldn't help yourself: floating
out of a Silurian sea, cell by matted cell
roused by the sun, blue-green

and blooming, lured to land where
you found feet and a backbone, roots,
leaves, seeds. You don't stop. Time

sashays like the wind, no mind to give it
word or grip or shape. None but
yours, Lucy, rocking in morning's cradle

as continents roll together and away, lock
each other in the mysteries of stone
and flood and molten sand. And oh,

the light. You open to it, limbs rhyming
in the air, your breath in the mist,
eyes beguiled by the dazzle above

the night. Billions of nights and moons,
and your dark skin begins to cover the earth
like silk, rising and falling. You lay

your milky gifts before the sun, again
and again, the arrow of dawn lodged deep
in your rib. Leave a bright marker

where they will find it, Lucy,
in the silt and ash of the ravines
of Ethiopia: hominid, woman. Later,

around a fire, in love with your dancing
bones, they imagine kaleidoscope
suns in the towering smoke

as they listen to a tune
on the camp radio. What name
can they give a find such as you?

2. And then, and still

eons pass, tumble into boxes, labelled. Cities bake in disease, the poison
of the Cloth heals and kills, guns and blood blossom in the desert
heat, earth turns warm and terrible under the rumble of drumming
feet. Still, you can't help yourself. You are the hungry kid under the wet
cardboard on the concrete, awakened by a crack of sun; a crone wrenching
her bottle cart from the melting ice; our daughters on the screen,
in the radiant wreckage of the light.

3. Here you are now

in the yeast of small, enthralling
fingers, scent that rises
from your skin. In a howl from your throat,

buds readying to be teeth. I measure
fear in volts as your fingers reach
for the frayed cord, as your unsteady feet try

the rocks, as each shadow in the park
turns menacing. I watch your eyes crackle
with spirit, your limbs stretch, see how your hip
juts into a new world
like a bowl or a fist. Soon, an empty room, abandoned
music, curled posters, your amulet in a silver box,

curtains translucent as moth wings. The sky,
its blue arms. Today, your voice on the phone, the arrow
of light lodged in our ribs. We can't help it, Lucy,

we are the memory of Hadar, its blue green
enchantment. We are its blooming and we rise
to our feet with the sun in our eyes.

You praise a blue dress

because she tells you the Chautauqua came to Shoal Lake the year
she was nine, and brown-haired Lillian and white-blonde Grace sat overlooking

the stage in the meeting house built by Carson, her grandfather,
and the organizers of the program plucked the two from the oak balcony

to model clothes—imagine! the thirties, and the abundance
of a moment when a stylish woman from the city turned to Grace:

"Dear," she said, "you need to wear rose and blue."
                                        And because
the year following, after her father died and Grace was sent to the McDonalds'

while her mother went to the city to train to be a nurse, Aunt Bell found
curtains, old clothing sent from Boston, anything to fashion

something rose, something blue for the white-blonde girl from an oak bluff
on the Western plains.

                    Because she tells you this now, over the phone
from her small and smaller apartment, and confesses she is afraid:

her father and Aunt Bell appear in dreams every night, as real to touch
as rough-hewn oak fashioned into a railing,

as a blue dress, empire-waisted, rose piping for trim.

Time after Time: Haibun for an old standard

Nicotine stains on her fingers, Ella on the player, cold tea on the table. She is back in her armchair in a housedress, eyes closed, skin strung over the clothesline of her bones. A thrush perches on the music: her voice. *"I only know what I know, the passing years will show"*—we danced *to that before we were married.* Outside, sun blazes on the snow, the sky dizzy with blue. *At the Fort Garry. I miss that.* I hang on her words, reach for her hand, the hospital bracelet orbiting her wrist. She sways to the melody, opens her eyes. *C'mon Mom,* I say, and she clings to my waist, rises, her misshapen feet like broken stairs. *Let's do this. You lead. "Time after time, you'll hear me say that I'm…"*

We stumble as we
step into the given—
this sad and slender song.

Hemlock Ravine

I walk the path of old
trees slapped down by high winds,

lying in grey huddles, praying
with brittle hands, broken

arms. Inert, their memories
of earth cracked apart in the fall.

Their reaches, once psalms against
rain, are sawn in angles, left

to dry. I climb over a trunk to pursue
something green; my legs like a spider's

crawl slowly, spiny and limber with
                        life. Oh, it was
so sudden. We had much more

to say to one another; we were
just learning the words.

Hillside Cemetery, Saskatoon

Forget God for a moment: consider the Latin *humanus,* human; *humere,*
to be moist; *humilis,* to be lowly; and *humus,* of the soil. We dig holes,
drop in bones, and for years afterward our feet trace paths between
tended grass and stones over all that lingers: loyalty, Annabel's ear for
music, Peter's unfinished argument and troubles with the gout, Eunice's
thick ankles, that Gallic pique. The dampness forming states of mind
as we traipse around in this short light: air, fire, water, and earth. And
you—remember those nights in the graveyard in the spring? How we
poured your father's rye into a thermos, tucked the afghan from your
mother's armchair under your parka, found a candle and two cigarettes.
We laughed to break down the dark, to hush stars, to claim dominion
over cold stone and whispers. *My soul to take.*

To the man upstairs

You son of a bitch: He was only sixteen.
Pure, quick limbs that surged the hill
on snow days with my son, swooping sleds

like low-flying kites. Joe Spirit, God, Big Guy,
whoever the hell: You butcher
hope. Morning brought a magpie, scolding

us, eating scattered seeds we left to keep
him from robbing a nest. The sun rose,
threw a rainbow across the valley flashing

every colour light can sing though glass. Good
trick, Jack, but cheap. You crack hearts
like eggs, track the shells through our veins.

Legs

Students criss-cross the intersection by the library,
hoodies unzipped, baggy jeans
low on their hips. Look: she wears tights and a short skirt, her eyes
wear the hungover look of thunder-clap sleep that follows love-making,
a green scarf puddles loosely around her neck, rope on a pier. She floats up, out
                              of slumber as though her limbs were cork,
moving in her skirt, the exact skirt she intended for the first hot day

—the curve of its cut, its bounce and sway, how it licks the air
the way the sea sifts out shadow––

and for all the days the sun will press its small moans and whispers
on her skin, all the mornings she can float on the improbable wave
of being twenty, her limbs free from winter's
tangled promises, smoky windows, reels of birds and gyres. She is ready,
to spring into the day, to spring into the days. Pilgrim,

she may be an oracle.

Winter fire on a country road

Spruce and alder have bled into dark, woodstoves are tamped down,
children in flannel, clocks ticking. A howl rips open the steep blue
wall of sleep, window crumpling with shredded light, and he rises,
feels the chill of his stiff boots by the door. In the black dazzle, sirens
are shrapnel in his ears, two-way radios squawk and buzz, gravel pops
under the grip of truck tires. Shaken, he picks his way over the ice to
where the red lights loop, where the curious have tumbled from their
houses and cars and line the road like torn packages: stricken hair,
parkas over pyjamas, head and hands bare, boots gaping, windows
down. A beehived woman with a child nuzzling into her coat sucks
hard on her cigarette, glassy sparks splinter. Beyond, a house blazes
like hallucination, gathers the circle of faces like strung moons, and he
joins—as though it were a campfire on the beach, the new barbecue
on the deck, the candle he lit in the bedroom overlooking the Codroy
that summer hoping he would get lucky. He joins as we all join when
we wonder what truth waits in the dark, what the devil offers this time,
which new play god is rehearsing. We don't know and who does, so,
clinging fiercely to our children, we lean closer into the rousing, divers
perched over hell's flowering heat. We open our coats: *forgive us.* We
ache to writhe inside such blue, lust so raw and ancient we can almost
see to the other side.

Home

The train's whistle pins me to the earth,
wheels shuffle and rattle the rails behind
the pines. The wind blows longing out of the hole
in my heart. I always fall

for the familiar. A concert of baritones in the Marysburg Church,
white and blue angels and saints on the walls,
"Beautiful Dreamer," "Amazing Grace," the harmonies
of August: flat road, dust, a harvest moon. All the tropes.

A hawk or two, the primary palette of canola, cloud,
and blood; painted ladies and clacking grasshoppers,
the geometries of wings opening, closing. Inside these
serial wonders, I am the middle of nowhere.

When they are old

days weigh like dust
thick on the leaves

of a roadside bloom.
Then: her fingertips,

his skin, the rain's
soft and trusting tongue.

When Puccini isn't enough
– after Tony Hoagland

Sometimes I wish I were still in Dauphin,
scavenging a snow-melt night for fresh
fire, driving down Main Street with Abbie, tuning in
to CKOM, Penny and Arlene in the back,
their hair-sprayed dos scraping

the inside roof of the car. And then:
Turn it up. Turn it up!
Don't they-ey know it's the end
of the world. Booster fuel for longing,
that old country music. We wanted

the dark, where we recognized cars
only by their headlights, guys by their
hands, the husk of their voices. To hide
in the open. Then, the next summer, the fuel
was rock, *hard.* How we wanted

—satisfaction, something
deeper, lighter. Anything beyond.
Now, decades and worlds later,
I pick up a guitar, learn three chords,
write a few lines, begin to sing:

Nothing to do when you've done all you can
Life happens in ways that you can't understand
Love comes and goes and it breaks you in two
There's nothing, just nothing you can do

Country, of course, and bad, but it's all right, a way
of shouldering the next season by
looping back to that spring at fifteen, its bright eye,

soft bone. The ache pouring from all those uncapped stars. And, yes, *caro*—all that singing in the dark.

Songs for Simone

Songs for Simone

We possess nothing in this world other than the power to say I. This is what we should yield up to God, and that is what we should destroy. – Simone Weil

Through all the tumult, and the strife/ I hear the music ringing;/ It sounds an echo in my soul—/ How can I keep from singing? – Traditional hymn

Trouvé 1.

> *The egg is this world we see, the bird*
> *in it is Love. When the shell is broken, the being*
> *is released, space is opened, torn apart. The spirit leaving*
> *is transported to a point which is not a point of view, but from which*
> *this world is seen.*

> *The moment stands still.*

> *The whole of space a dense silence, not*
> *absence, but sensation: the secret*
> *word who holds us in his arms from the beginning.*
> *The tree is rooted in the sky. A pearl buried*
> *deep in a field is not visible.*

> *Every dream of friendship*
> *deserves to be shattered. It is a miracle,*
> *like the beautiful. We must refuse*
> *it so that we may be worthy to receive it.*
> *It is of the order of grace.*

> *Workers need poetry more*
> *than bread. They need that their life*
> *should be a poem. They need light*
> *from eternity. Fall of the petals*
> *from fruit trees in blossom.*

J'offre 1.

Travel to Winnipeg with me, Simone, your voice on steel rails at dusk,
long ribbon of plainsong—in the morning, deer and the delicacy
of spring grass. Your ideas are a lens, sharp, hard, trapping light in anything

that moves. Your words urge me as I lift above the earth, resist gravity.
A sea of white foaming at 30,000 feet is cold leavening, blessing that invites
erasure, stirs a yearning to start from the beginning. On Portage Avenue,

wind outside the Bargain Centre. My brother and I reach for the car door-handle
when a man leans in, copper-sharp breath: *You think I want money, I won't ask
for money, just have a beautiful day*—can one ignore him?—

and below us, at the lip of a puddle: a penny, winking. We visit our mother who
snores in her high-rise bed, her mouth a dark field where, long ago, she buried
pearls. Your fingerprints everywhere on my imagination: the Big Dipper over

the alley behind Corydon, May snow cowering by the curb, air gathering thunder.
I want your ideas to rip at the flesh of my comfort. Later, coyote cantering
in the grass along the highway: intensity of raw sienna. Traffic is a metal trail

near the river; in the news, reports of a man looking under the hood struck down
by a car in front of his wife and two children. This is the meantime. When
I return home seeds I laid on the balcony are gone. Somewhere, because of this,

a bird lives. Simone, are we fools to hope when snow still flies? The virtue
of humility, you say, is nothing more or less than the power of attention. Detachment.
Purest is prayer, grace ascending, like wings. You take no bread, want to destroy

your power to say 'I.' Tell me, how to speak of you or for you without offering
the food of your creed, bread for the bellies of pilgrim spirits wandering
alone and far behind? How far can I travel with you?

J'imagine 1.

I read you and read you, but cannot understand the ferocity of your will. Catharism's appeal—its austerity, its doctrine of suicide by starvation. Belief that Satan created the physical world. Plato's wisdom, you say, offers an orientation of the soul toward grace. Musicians, poets, painters—you know he'd have them gone.

You love your truths more than life itself.

It is August, 1943. The Allied forces are embarrassed to find that the Japanese have slipped away from Kiska before they arrived. Duke Ellington plays Carnegie Hall for the first time. Northwest of Winnipeg, in the town of Neepawa on the Canadian prairies, Peggy Wemyss lands a job as a reporter and applies to United College, her novel about the costs of unflinching conviction still years ahead. Earlier that year, Dutch princess Juliana gives birth to her daughter in an Ottawa hospital, and the Canadian Government declares the room extra-territorial so that the child can retain her full Dutch citizenship. A little flexibility.

Death and hope are everywhere. Uprisings seize the Warsaw ghetto, the British have taken Tripoli from the Nazis, and a young woman from Rethymnon, Crete has just put the finishing touches on her wedding dress tatted from parachute silk. More than a year before, German soldiers had floated to the earth, abandoning their parachutes on the rocks among the goats. Adriani Antonakaki marries in her silk dress. There are many forms of resistance, including beauty. Every separation is a link, you say. Yet links can be loose, like limbs; they can be ways we move. To dance, we must let go.

In August of 1943, as you are dying, your young heart exhausted and starved and incandescent with love for God, a young woman is dancing to big band music at the Fort Garry, a railway hotel in downtown Winnipeg. Grace has come from the country to work in the Bank of Montreal where red-haired Jerry deposits his money, and on their first date—the night of the dance—she kills his family's pet bird. His parents live on one of those large tree-canopied streets in a spacious home with wooden columns. Grace is wearing a smart navy suit with a white blouse, and after introductions she sits on the chesterfield unaware the budgie has tucked itself behind the pillow.

Unaware. Decades later, as Grace is on her deathbed, she speaks of that bird. I imagine you on your last bed, Simone, smothered by hunger, thoughts thready, your pain rapturous, your bones delicate and brittle. Your mind is crippled by thirst and your tongue is swollen. Your breath is slow, your feet and hands cold. You will not ask for bread or water—you tell the doctors to send the food to France. Nor could your body take them now. In your state of decreating bliss are you now fully emptied? Is such perfection worth the price? Is someone there to bless you?

Trouvé 2.

1909, Paris: Simone Adolphine Weil, née 3 Fevrier, fille de Bernard et Selma. Ancestral faith: Jewish. Prophets: Marx and Freud.

1912, Paris: Maman Weil's word is law: *Wash, wash, wash your hands. Never allow yourself to be kissed. Send them on their way*, Maman said. Do you never wonder, Simone, about her obsession with cleanliness? her fear of touch?

1914: The kitchen table. You take a political stand. *Pas de sucre, Maman. It's not rationed to the soldiers.* Only five, and you have begun to refuse yourself, on principle.

1923: At fourteen you draw more lines; you want all or nothing. *My brother André is a genius, Maman, comme Pascal. I prefer to die rather than live outside the kingdom of truth reserved for genius.* Fate made you second-born, second-loved. Worse, a woman.

1924: So you make yourself unattractive. Emile Auguste Chartier says: *Tiens, Mlle Weil. You are my best student. But your hair covers your face, your suit is a man's, those are shoes too large, that cape bizarre. You do not wash. You do not clean your teeth. You are a Martian.* You say: *I am the colour of dead leaves, like certain unnoticed insects. Touche pas.*

You see man-woman as a struggle for power. You say all power is soiled. It is filth. You say: *The family is legalized prostitution, the wife is a lover reduced to slavery.* If you can't be loved, you don't want it. Convictions, truths: we find many ways to raise our fists at pain.

1938: Ah, but song finds you. In an abbey in Solesmes, the Gregorians, singing as a way of tuning the universe, aligning the notes of your soul. You write:

Here at the Benedictine Abbey of Solesmes, here at the moment when my migraine was at its worst, I have experienced the bitterness of Christ's passion as a real event. Mystical revelation. I have found faith without losing my suffering…a pure and perfect joy in the beauty of the chanting and the words…

You refuse to be baptized. You want to be, in your words, *an exile in relation to every human circle without exception.* The principality of Simone has edicts, laws.

J'offre 2.

I find direction in your words: *attention, to its highest degree, is prayer. We must empty ourselves in order to be filled.* Virginia Woolf wrote that the shock-receiving capacity is what makes her a writer—the shock, then the desire to explain it. To be pierced with wonder in the everyday is what entices me. It empties me and it fills me. I am struck by your devotion, frightened by your inflexibility, curious about the depth of your anger. Can I slice my complacency to the bone, as you have, and still sing?

I want to offer you something. This is difficult. My words seem inadequate: cheap trinkets discarded in Piazza San Marco, a plastic wreath on an altar in Notre Dame.

Limited, stained by gravity, I am one who would be banished, but who thrives on song. I would offer you Robert Johnson or Emmy Lou Harris, the strains of "O Mio Babbino Caro," "Simple Gifts," soaring gospel. Songs whispered on ships or ringing from the factory door at closing time. A song is beauty, earthed, is it not? You have written that beauty is eternity here below: our contract with beauty a sacrament.

I put down your words, turn on the radio: more innocents are hunted down by tumescent forces. I think of you, red virgin, of your words for this unrest: undeveloped, primitive. *La pesanteur:* gravity. You said once: *Gasoline is much more likely than wheat to be a cause of international conflict.* And: *A nation cannot be the object of supernatural love. It has no soul. It is a Great Beast.* You were right. About many things, you were right.

And I realize I am reading you because I am blind, feeling for the walls of belief. I too want belief so deep it will swallow me. *Just give me one thing to hold on to/ To believe in this living is just a hard way to go...*

So, to start with, I hold on to song. It's all I wish to hold, and all I can offer.

J'imagine 2.

Italy, 1937: In the little chapel Santa Maria degli Angeli where Saint Francis had prayed, you kneel because you are drawn by something stronger, you say, *than I.* In 1938, you write a young student named Jean Posternak to say you heard "Figaro," that you were overtaken by the Incoronazione di Poppea in the Boboli Gardens amphitheatre under the stars, the Pitti Palace in the background. *Music of such simplicity, serenity, and sweetness, of such dancing movement,* you write. I imagine you, your flight into pure joy. Reading your words, I think of music as linguistics of the spirit, a craning toward harmony with God. I think of all the bridges we cross. Isn't music, even played or sung off-key, our attempt to play the notes of another shore?

The Brooklyn Bridge. London Bridge. The Ponte Vecchio. You crossed a bridge that day in Florence toward, as you say, *pure and perfect joy.* In 1943, Billie Holliday, addicted to heroin and opium, was making one thousand dollars a week. The pure and perfect "God Bless the Child" was supporting the young woman born Eleonora Fagan Gough, descendant of slaves, raped at the age of ten. In 1943, when you died, Eunice Kathleen Waymon, the girl who grew to be Nina Simone—*I want a little sugar in my bowl*—made her concert debut as a pianist, refusing to play until her parents were seated, along with white folk, at the front of the room.

Billie, Nina, Grace. Peggy. Juliana. Adriani. Simone.

More bridges. I try to imagine your reaching to hold a man or a woman, finding a little sugar in your bowl. Yet when I imagine your lover, I imagine only my advice, impoverished and too late.

I would say this: Simone belongs to no one. Her knowing is the one raven can respect. She longs, but not for your footsteps, and she burns, but with indifference to your glance. It happens, you know. Don't try *I want you I need you you're my baby my baby.* Dismantle the possessive, unhinge the transitive: let that caboose loose to rest by the siding. You dream of Simone, you imagine yourselves together on a street in Boulogne-Billancourt where you're drinking absinthe—*bien sur*—in a brasserie by the river. Tea and oranges will come later, you hope. It's payday at the foundry and your hands are red as the blood of Christ from pulling hot metal bobbins for the metro from the furnace, and you want Simone. She asks you, *What if Eve, overwhelmed with desire*—o yes, you think, and she continues—*what if Eve refused to eat the apple?*

(*I love to you* is what Irigaray will say years later—close enough, but neither of you knows this now. Nor would you care; you're hungry and Simone wants only to smoke, not eat, and night is falling. She ignores the music. The waiter is impatient.)

O dear imperfect soul, you can't take this woman, and you can't leave her. She is God's alone. Her heart is a subject that needs no object: love is its own fire and a raven can be so deeply blue the moon will swallow it in the dark.

Trouvé 3.

Your voice, Simone, in a chorus of others'—Chuang Tzu, Lao Tzu, the Desert Fathers, philosophers, poets.

Fall of the petals from fruit trees in blossom.

Looking is what saves us.

We need our lives to be a poem.

The wise are good at letting go.

J'offre 3.

What if the search for the divine *is* a search for song? Hermes hollowed out the tortoise shell to create the lyre. Simone, you hollowed out yourself to be with God. You became the song.

> *Some bright morning when this life is over,*
> *I'll fly away.*
> *To a home on God's celestial shore,*
> *I'll fly away.*

J'imagine 3.

1943: A prairie ballroom, big band music in the middle of the war, a young woman dancing in spite of what she has destroyed. A blues singer, a factory worker, a writer, a bride. Imagine all these as the chanting of the world. And none will last. Perfection, joy, genius, edicts—they fray, become unravelled. Eggs crack open. Moments stand still. We are all songs of imperfection; everything is how we imagine it; we are as orphaned as clouds.

And we possess nothing.

This is the meantime.

> *Through all the tumult and the strife*
> *I hear the music ringing;*
> *It sounds an echo in my soul—*
> *How can I keep from singing?*

Just so you know

Winter kill

The vanes of the feather placed like a talisman
on the windowsill turn toward the pines fringing
the field, sad gods known only to themselves.

The snow sharpens its cold notes on their needles.
To love is to pity: this is the beginning
and the end of all there is

to know. The field is scalloped in drifts, and the deer taken
down by their throats; their ribs, cleaned by claw
and tooth, curve around the weight

of absence. Here is where we teach the spirit
to move into sorrow the way a field dissolves,
meltwater, into spring.

Driving at night

It's hard now, says Susan as she pours another few ounces of red,
the oncoming lights are so intense. Frank says put that on the list,
and leans back in his chair, closes his eyes. Outside, a plough roars,
impressing its cold fretboard in the road, the street light swirls a crystal
world, edgeless and doorless and moonless but for the old pine, an
apparition long ago widowed by birds. You heard about Pat, didn't
you? Jean winces, shifting in her chair; her sciatica. Pat's one of the
few who look good bald, I think. A wig costs so much, says Maureen,
and she can't stand them, so I knit her a hat instead. Her twentieth
round—how can she do it? Siren in the street; tinkling glass inside.
From the quiet end of the table, Bill says: The trickster. Throws
everything at us. We turn to look—the creases in Bill's eyes darken in
candlelight. The plate of roast chicken is shredded remnants; crusty
bits of skin, a wing. Frank pushes away his salad. Does everything have
to mean? Maureen picks at a loose thread in the napkin. I'll call a cab
later. You'd better open another bottle. It may be March, but it's clear
there's no let-up. A toast to the snow.

St. Boniface

They walked out, coats unbuttoned at thirty-five below,
stepped around smokers who stood outside the atrium by the revolving
doors—shots of warmth along with their nicotine—past trees
triumphantly lit on the boulevard, past taxis,

emergency vehicles, a woman in a light jacket shielding a child
and clutching a suitcase, everyone with a hundred-yard
stare. And with their shoes scuffing ice and salt, they crossed
over to the park to search for the car they brought—was it

only that morning? Somewhere around here. Snow had blown
across the diagonal path so they made their own, heads down,
tracking each other's feet. Nothing now but that
small focus. Behind them, the cross on the hospital roof

was a beacon—against cold, despair; or for salvation perhaps—
and it cast light on the backs of the four as they, unaware, fell into step
in birth order across the field. One held a bag with a nightdress. They walked
slowly in the dark, like shepherds in drifts, away from miracles.

Just so you know

You will feel awkward, as though emerging from the dark
with lime green hair, your eyes rumoured to be radioactive.

Someone will mention angels, better rewards, another will channel
the sticky wisdom of a country song about new stars in the sky,

the significance of certain dates. Three crows. Or the doctor's slip
of the tongue. Redemption written into the final clutch of a hand.

What you thought were vapours of the fantastic harden, herniate
the everyday: she knew or he knew, or you, surely, must have known.

Must have known. Like Jesus on the wall of the Tim Horton's,
there were signs, yes, there were signs.

Just so you know. You won't. They didn't. There weren't. Meaning
is what you try to wear like tight black shoes you found

in a rush at the thrift store because you hadn't planned
on a funeral, greeting the forgotten, your startling green hair drawing

words from others' mouths as they avert the danger
in your eyes: I'm sorry, they say, I'm sorry, you must be, you must

be, and you walk as carefully as anyone who is blistering
can walk, impossibly, carrying hot tea in a cup across a room

roaring with the mortal who reach now for pinwheel
sandwiches, pickles. Perhaps one of those nice Nanaimo bars.

Address for the dead

…far away, points of light.
— Tomas Tranströmer

They leave too soon: small battles,
small white rooms. And we huddle, bewildered,
our tongues stunted. But what if there

were a train in a mountain valley, its steam
seething, waiting? Everything still. A black
itinerary on the wall free of chalk,

ticket cage abandoned. We would dally,
of course, drop things, but board anyway, hoping
to ride, swaying, across hills

and bridges like memory, the trestle
we've built for time. Rails of shot light ahead
and behind where we hope

to reach one another. After all,
we've been responsible, haven't we? Faithful to
silver trails bristling with intention, waltzing

all that moonstuff into morning, making baskets
of purpose, giving them away?
Oh, please. We are

jackals, alone in the godforsaken woods, scrabbling
for blood in a potter's ground, roots dangling
from our claws. We ignore any

sound that will not feed us. Howl,
prick our mange in the underbrush. Lights we follow
are blunted and diffuse

as raw-boned need. Yes, too soon they go,
and go, and are gone, as quickly as the tracks swallow
trains, horizons. The idea of after.

Spring again

Rain washed away most of the snow yesterday, the day
to change clocks. Drops didn't fall so much as urged—
it's time, they murmured, pushing warm fingers into sullen

drifts. Along Lacewood, faded cellophane and streaked
papers clinging to the verge between curb
and stone wall, leftovers of the local expressions

of condolence to the widow of a man pinned
there by a newly licensed teenage driver. A skinny
girl in green rubber boots toes in, uphill, clasping

fingers of a long-legged young man with low-riding pants
and big white shoes: *keep on truckin'*, an old Big Brother
and the Holding Company album comes to mind. This

could be spring, odours of rot rising from October's leaves,
tires spritzing, and the bright air hardening—the wind
working, too, on this devotion to movement,

to washing away. Spring intends, regardless:
a friend appears at meetings to work on policies that will
outlive her, and another says she rarely calls because

she has worn out her terminal-illness welcome,
has persevered four years, losing hair and growing it,
losing it again—why is it always a battle, she asks, and why

must it always be courageous; what do I do now
with more daylight, another celebration of crocuses?
Dogs on the path sniff strangers, squat, wind worries

the puddles, ice by the tracks becomes pliable
and pocked. Crows flap like clergy into bare
limbs along the road: it all goes on. We are all wild

pieces of some whispering heart, moving inside light
and dark, the soles of our shoes damp
and leaking. But we move, *cry cry baby*,

our steps precise slaps on wet streets, eyes
alert for the spark of red still trapped
in last year's leaf. Its gritty spine.

Father Martin

Under the steady feet of brothers, underneath stained glass, pews, and ceremonies smooth as the sonorous notes of the organ, he cared for the books: 1559. 1565. 1882. The Old World in steamer trunks and church habiliments, tumbled in dust and optimism across candescent miles of grass and faith. God help us all. Bones of the ancestors tilt on the shelves, mute antiphon for a distant choir. Tucked into a cover, a misspelled plea from the priest from Shaunavon, a century gone: *I am loosing gradually. Remember me.* Beyond the elms, under the crescent scar containing time, three deer draw light from the field along the east, and across the tracks, a coyote strips the cry from the throat of a fledgling hawk.

Not alone

All afternoon I sit under the eaves behind the house with
      rain pressing its cold nose at my neck, self-pity sidling up
            against me, clutching its sour belly. I'm never alone.

Monks are shot in the streets of Burma, the war bill rings
      into trillions, and the old ficus by the fireplace
            has no mind, no beating heart, but it too is dying.

We bought organic potatoes at the market, sliced them open—
      give me spots on my apples, leave me the birds and the bees—
            felt milky juice, saw braids of rot tied at the centre.

In the box in the closet—what he left when he was leaving her: a note—
      I will give you $250 a month for groceries, one piece of tail a week.
            Then I washed and washed the anger from my hands.

If I think of gods as nets I weave myself, what do I think
      I'll catch? I need only air, blood, water. Yet don't I need words
            that make the gods? Oh, snake, you eat your tail.

In the urgency of lists and mail and food and taxes my desire to see
      the moon can vanish. And watch out, an old woman reminds me,
            a finger's blind unless the moon is shining.

Rain may have small hands but not on this coast; here, it raises
      brass knuckles, pisses off the wind and I brace against
            bitterness, inconsolable.

Silence pins me to the bed until morning clears its throat, rises.
      I hunker in a crowd of shadows as the surge of traffic beats
            the air. This wide world. You: not here.

The biting

Leaves had fallen, still bright against our feet, but damp
and browning. Wind had clawed away the wall of green

so that we could see the water, feel its ancient grey eye.
We drove into the yard just as he came up the stairs

from the back garden, an armful of buckets and tools,
a patterned rug, and thrust toward me a small framed image: Here—

you would appreciate this, he said. Two beetles etched on birch bark,
exquisite points where tooth had met the skin of tree. His voice

keen, softening, and about to break: I have no idea who
gave it to her, or when. None. The leaves were dervishes

around us, the sun had gone. My friend busied herself
with the key, the trunk. I raised my arm to embrace

him, but he leaned into the car, placed with care
garden forks, pails of seed packets, rug, then turned

toward the backyard, head down. This is hard, I wanted
to say, these last things. A gust, and several envelopes tumbled

from a pail into the air, skittering across the driveway to land
near bowed plants, wild with overgrowth, as she had been

at the end. I rushed to gather them. *Feverfew: planted March 27,*
2005, written in her small, careful hand. *Verbascum nigrum:*

planted March 25, 2006. Astrantia Major. Ruby Cloud.
Corbeille d'argent. Grief has more seeds than flowers do, I thought,

as I watched him disassemble a cold frame, and one is our
not knowing the provenance of small things

the other has loved. Against my chest, the framed Cree biting
that will remind me. Around us, the wind reeling, circling,

its cold teeth precise as devotion, impressing
the remains of a garden in fall.

Dusk

is such a ragged time. The shirred day loosened from the line we strung
across the reach of morning, when a bird called out its signature, its signature,
and we opened to the hours ahead, settling in to carve again a pure
clear shape around each thought and plan, an offering, a duty done,
a passage read, or one more step or image caught or lesson learned or heart
set right, but sundown pulls along its arc the last descending string of light,
leaves us with minutes in our hands, frayed recollections, wild release,
the folly of ambitious plans we trade for rest and abject peace.

Horse

A star followed me to the end of the dark road where I found a horse.
I had set out for an evening walk. Behind me was a field, behind the
field, a mountain. In the indigo above the mountain, a star, my bright
companion. As were the dogs—did I mention the quiet husky, the
curious, frantic pup? Did I mention the green hallways of vineyard
beside the road? But I was telling you about the horse, his presence
dark and heavy as the smell of his coat. Having startled each other,
we called out, each in our own language. He allowed my hand to pat
his sturdy neck, my fingers to stroke his nose, but neither of us moved
closer. This was not the night to ride. The wind had already dropped
her invisible scarves somewhere on the field. Trees and birds were
quiet. The dogs kept their distance. I tell you the only truths I know.
It was dark. A star followed me. I found a horse. I did not ride.

Incantation

Cold spring wind, Sheila's Brush and
middens of tissue, word, and bone.

Moon: pull down memory.

May three deaths be taken from you;
three ages given you.

Songs gather in villages when they are not sung.
They swim in lakes, waiting to be caught. They spin
out of silver constellations, and wait in shadow.

Come back, song.
Come back as good tidings, as rhapsody.

Listen, winter traveller:
a small gust will beckon, drain you of promises, fill you
with old music, mournful as the Pleiades and as far away.
When it arrives in the evening, allow its golden hem
to brush against you.

You will be sung in the morning.
You will be gathered and sung in the morning.

Seven daughters rise from the sea;
four winds hurry grass on the plains.
Moon: pull down memory.
Small-throated griefs, fly away.

Small-throated griefs, fly away.

Comes a time

Denying, believing, doubting is to men what running is to horses. – Blaise Pascal

Night borders

It's a big country, and we are always learning to arrive or leave.
Each trip a glimpse of a hand plunging into water: *something down there,*
and we want it found. Rapid eye movements—a hotel operator calling back,
but we hang up, or a poet in a pub in Wadena wearing a long scarf,
and raising a glass to grief. This terminal
of changelings behind our eyes: every night crowded
with frowns from a photograph a son sent, perhaps, or the grin
of a forgotten lover through a crack in the door. The rose room, the clip
that cannot hold papers falling from our hands. We can't remember—
images shuffle like face cards, fly apart. We can't track this country;
it's our lonely planet. All tremble and flicker, like silver grass
or iridescent tails of fish we might have seen, or will.

Hubbards Cove

A melting tune. Sun bebops over the trees, dogs erupt, icicles swoon,
the drainpipes jazzed by their trickling scat. I bump the bed covers
down the stairs, puffs of cat hair winking in the astonishment of light,
haul them over the line, bite their stale winter skins with pins as the
wind rips up the driveway, snatches the ends of the covers, and lifts—

                     like paper off a thundering cliff,
gulls' long banking, parachuting nuns, hovering carpets humming, up
and up and the top of my bed suspended between woodshed and pine
and the throng of spring glitter, sun and wind lindy-hopping. Lyric
I can ride. What else but to slip out of my soggy wool socks, feel bare
feet on the cool-slick porch, breathe in, climb aboard?

They say reason alone

will thwart wild children, daydreaming, and reckless
expression. Cognition will line them all up in rows, snap

his phone shut, grab his briefcase, chuck chins
on the way out the door. All you wanted was to become

lost. October: a red leaf rides home on the sole of your boot
and you peel it off, regretting it will not enter the ground

where it grew. Nothing stays put: even eggplant takes
a refrigerated trip from Mexico to your plate. Think

of those blue streams of silence where birds and moons
are hidden, and the long boat of your blood

glides away into mouths of even longer rivers. Maverick
hearts, harmonic fifths, bright tapestries align; nothing

subtracts or wants an audit or a goal or a password.
Glad tidings arrest you there as this leaf has here—

startling you with notes of red and gold. A place beyond the idea
of photosynthesis, beyond this tree and shore-hung forest—

a place where you can wade into the birth of everything,
witchy and languorous. Released.

Wild

All night you hear the birds, hundreds of them, restless,
erupting, their racket filling the meadow, mocking
the mountain, the cold-stone calm of the old
paperbark tree. What force opens their throats? What promise
has been broken, what currents of hope and fear
rush through those fragile bones, spring into their eyes,
batter blood through the small devices of their hearts?
Listen,
              nothing lasts. Quiet can be stolen like your bag
in the street. You will soon be awake in all the wrong places,
your words snatched out of time. Oblivion is a wise
old teacher: *there is no try.* It's all right. You didn't get it
until this moment, did you? Wake every chance you can, join
the chorus, praise the wild. Carry light.

That spring

I was much further out than you thought
And not waving but drowning.
— Stevie Smith

April night: rushing clouds. You toss, leavening under wool, as the cat
curls around her ball of sleep. The moon casts light
                          from elsewhere, an ocean of presence.
Somewhere a cave: thin boys with olive skin crawl
with fear, someone offers up another girl child
                          to that thing with feathers. A body is lifted,
another raw red spurt of terror. Somewhere, breakfast over plans
for bombs, a continent left to bake in disease. You are another
bonehouse, drifting on ruins
of fortune, craving only sleep, oblivious to undertow.

Turn

Something happens late July when a cool wind
gushes through the screen, reminds me the season

has peaked, dandelion and thistle have scattered
their future in white puffs, and the sun has dragged me

along the days until evening—earlier now, simmered
and drawn, sweet butter. Reminds with each berry

and grasshopper what happens to love and regret, and what
grace can grow in the blue plum of summers that reappear

each year. Deeper, and I didn't have to ask. Each a cell
inside a cell, a pulsing arc—my mother's hand reaches

from my body to cradle tomatoes as my grandmother's
ruffles the Selkirk ground for a four-leaf, as her mother's

plucks vein-blue saskatoons near Norway House, each of us
touching berry, leaf, fruit, drawing

blood from the soil, drawing still. Deeper,
and we didn't have to ask.

Second-hand philosophy

It's a day to listen to country music at the local thrift store, wearing
the soft corduroy shirt with the funky smell you don't want to wash
out. A day to pick through the racks and overhear the young woman
with the wail in her voice talk about her night course. *I was kicked out
of the other one*, she says, leaning over the table to the clerk
with the aimless eyes who is sorting shirts into long sleeves and short;
*I was kicked out for—what did they call it?—confidentiality. I said things
out loud I shouldn't have. I need to learn to write it down
or keep it in my head.*

It's a day for separating sleeves by length, shirts by colour, for wondering
where to draw the lines that shape us, between what we think
and what we tell. To wonder about detours, small divinities—the aisle
that holds red and orange polyester dresses with bent foam shoulder pads
that someone once wore to a dance, perhaps, felt beautiful. Or the two-chord
tune that urged us to ride our horse, *darlin'*, to *dream that dream*. Tales that fell apart,
tidings that can't be gentled into story, cannot slip easily over our hips. Bright
broken buttons we wear out loud.

Writing has always felt like praying
— Reverend Ames

Gotama saw the face of his infant son and sleeping wife,
shaved his head and beard, put on his yellow robe,
and left without saying goodbye. Duties, possessions,
ties of the heart: all dust
weighing down his soul. He walked and walked,
seeking a life wide open, complete and pure as a polished shell.

In a cave away from the fray of Mecca, vendettas,
and a world soured by commerce, Muhammad
shook as the words of a new scripture
came to him. Surrendered himself
to its beauty, singing and weeping verse by verse, year by year
for twenty-one years.

Of course you remember the man from Galilee
who carried on his back the very wood on which
his blood was spilled. How he pushed back the rock
from the front of the cave and—this is gospel—
ascended, emptied of self and full of god, returning
now in offerings of bread and wine.

I pace back and forth on a cliff above the unknowable, lured
by slippery and maverick tales that call forth terror, crack
the earth, shatter my bones with light. I have no need
to verify old brown marks of stigmata, translate Coptic fragments.
A burlap robe on display in the cold stone air of the Church of Santa Croce
is inscrutable: it tells me only that my body is a ragged garment
and will be discarded too.

But here, now, I am ready as a tuned string
to witness what is ravenous, mythic. Here I am holy, misbegotten,
gossip on the lips of the gods, forgotten by the time the cups
are washed and put away. So I start as I start every day,
cobbling a makeshift pulpit, casting for truths as they are given me:
man, woman, child, sun, moon, breath, tears, stone, sand, sea.

After a full day

walk out in the afternoon, blue
steeping and the ripe pear light
splayed
on the gravel road. A monarch
braves the stall line,
goldenrod lolls. Feet,
their small uproar. Something is left
unsaid here. September,
                              and everything
aches
as red crawls into the leaves: elegance
in the sway of the old
man on the road, his drooping
suspenders, his hunchbacked love

for the small dog
with the Groucho Marx face.
The lithe movement of this season, insisting
I taste the bitter
end of what I thought

I wanted. The best time,
it is, the best, and I tilt back
my mouth, suck in the thick brew
of dust and wild mustard, invite
the sun to spike the water
in my eyes.

You think of Meister Eckhart

as the wind rises in the eucalyptus, follows tunnels of light
the queltehue have shaped in the air, tunnels that disappear inside

their own creation. Breath is to story as running is to horses, all wild eyes
and urgency, dust and dream flank, rush of imagination. And you wonder:

how does she find her way with those invisible hands? But when she whispers
at night as you try to steer stars, you wake with only the taste of the answer

in your mouth. And you think of Jesus, of the Buddha, of St. Teresa,
of the poet who drank wine from blue goblets, wrote

green lines on driftwood, slept with women he kept mistaking for the sea.
Can you learn to be empty as a clay pot, to be that simple,

that lavish?
         —and you walk on seashells among angels and devils, away

from lanzas and pirates whose treasures won't last, and you tap
your small crystal heart with the lightstick of the world, and listen:

you know music cannot be as sharply drawn as the eyes of a captive hawk, nor
pinned down to staves with clefs and a rest. It is bird-shriek at dawn, chug-

churning engines hot with promise, murmuring cows that trail swollen udders,
generous whispers of the fig tree summer-heavy with fruit you break open

in your palm and lay on your tongue. It is what you have already known
and tasted, mystery that grows in tears and bone, in death and rock and ocean,

the space on the stairs between this step and the next, in the red muscle
of mercy. It longs and it is longing and it wants you as virgin, wants you

as wife, lover, child, over cloud, under water, wants your throb
and blood-thirst, buried tears, and more. It shows you that soft is stronger

than hard, that you—rapt listener, ripening soul—always knew how to dance
this river, this winter, to compose out of the distant cry of stars.

Faith

…that's how we kept what we gave away.
– Neil Young

Uncertainty is the truth,
says the ajahn; sit and wait
for nothing to grow
but the small fire in your ears
which you can feed with anything you find nearby:
birdsong, perhaps, or the echoes
of trouble. Desire. Until the smoke
has cleared. Until everything goes.

The old country of awareness
has no record of your name.
Your name. You would do well
to give that up, too.

Notes and Sources

Many of these poems, or versions of them, have been published (in print, online, or broadcast) in the following anthologies, journals, and media: *Arc, CV2, Third Floor Lounge, 100 Poets Against the War* (ed. Todd Swift), CBC Radio One (Nova Scotia), *To Find Us: Words and Images of Halifax, Common Magic (poems for Bronwen Wallace), White Ink, The Society,* and *Learning Landscapes,* among others. A section of "Lost gospels" earned honorable mention in *Arc*'s 2007 International Poem of the Year contest.

Italicized opening lines in "Verge" are from Trevor Herriot's *River in a Dry Land* (Toronto: Stoddart, 2000, p. 155 (a quote from John Macoun's journal has been slightly modified to make tense consistent)); and from Bonnie J. Lawrence and Anna L. Leighton's *Prairie Phoenix: The Red Lily in Saskatchewan* (Regina: Nature Saskatchewan, 2005, p. 103 (authors) and p. 63 (Frank Pfeiffer)).

"Time after Time" (1947) was written by Sammy Cahn and Jule Styne.

References in "Songs for Simone" include:
   Weil, Simone (1979). *Gravity and Grace.* With an introduction by
      Gustave Thibon (trans. Arthur Wills). New York: Octagon
      Books (Division of Farrar, Straus and Giroux). Copyright, 1952.
   Weil, Simone (1951). *Waiting on God: The Essence of her Thought.*
      London: Collins (Fontana Books).
   Miles, Sian (1986). *Simone Weil: An Anthology.* London: Virago Press.
   Wright, Charles, in Zwicky, J. (2003). *Wisdom & Metaphor.* Kentville,
      NS: Gaspereau Press.

Songs referred to in "Songs for Simone" include "Angel from Montgomery," John Prine. c. 1971; "I'll Fly Away," Albert E. Brumley c. 1932; "How Can I Keep from Singing," Robert Lowry lyrics, c. 1860; excerpts from Leonard Cohen's "Suzanne."

The found poem (*Trouvé 1*) comprises Weil's words from source materials.

"Spring again" is in memory of Pat Clifford, "The biting" in memory of Patricia Baker, "Hillside Cemetery, Saskatoon" in memory of Gordon Larson, "To the man upstairs" in memory of Edward Snair, and "Just so you know" and "Not alone" are in memory of Grace Glenn Boggs.

"Lost gospels: 8" is for Kay Reynaud.
"Night borders" is for Don McKay.
"When Puccini isn't enough" is for Rose Vaughan.
"St. Boniface" is for Allison, Brian, and Ron.

Acknowledgements

I owe a debt of gratitude to Marnie Parsons for her fine editorial eye, to Barry Dempster for his encouragement and faith, to the remarkable Alayna Munce for her gifted and astute copy-editing, and to Maureen Scott Harris and Don McKay for inspiring conversations and careful readings of versions of "Songs for Simone." Friends whose listening and support enriched these poems include Tracy Hamon, Stan Dragland, Maureen Scott Harris, Kathy Mac, Alex Pierce, Anne Simpson, Mary Jane Copps, Trevor Herriot, Barbara Langhorst, Robert LeBlanc, Dave Margoshes, Cynthia French, Rose Vaughan, and the writers of St. Peter's Abbey and Los Parronales. I am grateful for the work of the talented Brick team, including Alan Siu and the marvel that is Kitty Lewis. Thank you to my sons, Jesse and David, and to Allison, Brian, and Ron. My deepest thanks go to Allan Neilsen, whose steadfast love, timely wit, and great coffee bring me joy.

Lorri Neilsen Glenn is the author of three previous collections of poetry, including *Combustion* (Brick Books, 2007). An award-winning ethnographer and essayist, she is the author and editor of six books on research and literacy, a forthcoming collection of essays on loss, and an anthology about mothers. Poet Laureate for Halifax from 2005-2009, Lorri lives and works in Halifax, and returns often to the Prairies where she was born.